THE JEWELER'S SHOP

THE JEWELER'S SHOP

A Meditation on the Sacrament of Matrimony,
Passing on Occasion into a Drama

KAROL WOJTYLA

Translated from the Polish by Boleslaw Taborski

Random House
New York

Library of Congress Cataloging in Publication Data
John Paul II, Pope, 1920–
The jeweler's shop.
"First appeared in Poland under Wojtyla's
literary pseudonym, Andrzej Jawien, in the
December 1960 issue of the Catholic monthly, Znak."
A play.
Translation of Przed sklepem jubilera.
1. Marriage—Drama.
PG7169.04P713   891.8'5'27   79-5543
ISBN 0-394-51031-3

Manufactured in the United States of America
24689753
First Edition

Design by Bernard Klein

Acknowledgments

My humble gratitude is due to the author for having inspired me with the wish to translate his dramatic works from the Polish original.

I am indebted to Sister Emilia Ehrlich for her comments, to Mike Simpson for having looked over the text, and to Carol O'Brien of Hutchinson, the British publisher, for her efficient help in the preparation of the final version of this translation.

B.T.

CONTENTS

INTRODUCTION

Speaking to the intellectuals and artists of his old metropolitan See of Krakow during his historic journey to Poland in June 1979, Pope John Paul II recalled that one of the closest friends of his youth "considered the spoken word and the theater to be my calling, but Our Lord Jesus thought it was priesthood." The future Pope's connections with the theater, in one way or another, spanned well over three decades, and for some of that time it was an open question in which of the two directions young Karol Wojtyla would go. The theater had been his great passion since childhood in the town of Wadowice, where he was the star actor in numerous school productions, some of which he also helped direct. And it remained a passion in his student days at Krakow, both before and during World War II, when he was a member of three theater groups in succession.

It was in 1941 that Karol Wojtyla's theatrical aspirations were realized most fully. In that year he co-founded, with Dr. Mieczyslaw Kotlarczyk (the friend recalled four decades later in the Pope's speech), the Rhapsodic Theater, in which he was one of the acting company of five. One of the best groups in the Polish resistance at the time of the German occupation, the Rhapsodic Theater staged mainly poems and dramas of the great Polish romantics, inspired by their poetic imagery and by their intensely patriotic as well as metaphysical qualities. Wojtyla remained with the Rhapsodists until he turned from philological to theological studies and began to prepare himself for priesthood in the closing years of the war.

In his first years as a priest, Karol Wojtyla organized theatrical activities in the parishes where he worked and very occasionally still acted himself. He maintained ties with his friends of the Rhapsodic Theater right up to the time of his elevation to the papacy, and—under a nom de plume—reviewed their performances even as an archbishop.

One of the most significant and durable manifestations of Karol Wojtyla's interest in the theater was playwriting. It originated almost as early as his poetry, and, in fact, his plays showed a close affinity with his poems, though over the years their style underwent a considerable evolution. First came poetic dramas on Biblical themes. By Christmas 1939 the nineteen-year-old Wojtyla had written a drama, *David*, followed at Easter 1940 by another in the same vein, *Job*. At about this time he also finished a new Polish translation of Sophocles' *Oedipus*. By the summer of 1940 another play, called *Jeremiah*, was ready; in this he began to experiment both with different poetic styles and with dramatic structure, linking the Biblical theme to events in seventeenth-century

Polish history. In the late 1940s Father Wojtyla (as he was then) went back to playwriting. He wrote a play in prose, entitled *Our God's Brother*, perhaps more of a stage play than his others. It retold in dramatic form the story of Adam Chmielowski, a talented nineteenth-century painter who gave up art and (as Brother Albert) founded a religious congregation caring for the poor. Later the literary writings of Bishop Wojtyla entered what might be called his pastoral phase. As far as drama is concerned, two works belong in this period: *The Jeweler's Shop* and a play that continues some of its themes and is written in a similar style, *The Radiation of Fatherhood—A Mystery.*

Karol Wojtyla never cared much about the publication of his literary output. This is most clearly exemplified by the fate of his dramatic works. Before he was elected to the papacy, none had been performed and only one had been published. *The Jeweler's Shop* appeared under his most frequent literary pseudonym, Andrzej Jawien, in the December 1960 issue of the Catholic monthly *Znak* (The Sign) in Krakow. Subtitled "A Meditation on the Sacrament of Matrimony, Passing on Occasion into a Drama," it is in fact both a meditation and a poetic drama, with some scenes in prose and with excerpts from letters. There is also a chorus, which appears twice: a chorus of witnesses to a marriage, commenting on the action and offering a lyrical reflection on the union of two people, and the dangers inherent in it, not unlike the choruses in Greek tragedy. The lines of the chorus are short, the poetic imagery more direct than in the rest of the play.

For the most part, however, the play is written in long lines of free-flowing blank verse of changing rhythms and uneven numbers of syllables. At a casual glance the play reminds one of the easy conversational style which marked T. S. Eliot's later plays. It is the impression one forms from the very first lines, where Teresa says:

Andrew has chosen me and asked for my hand.
It happened today between five and six in the afternoon.

But this "conversational ease" is deceptive. The writing here, as in his poems, is in fact compact, often turning into semi-philosophical or moral discourse, laden with symbols relating to the central theme of betrothal and marriage, as well as to the nature of man. The jeweler's speech on the latter subject (quoted by Andrew) is a good example of the density of the imagery:

Ah, the proper weight of man!
This rift, this tangle, this ultimate depth—
this clinging, when it is so hard
to unstick heart and thought.
And in all this—freedom,
a freedom, and sometimes frenzy,
the frenzy of freedom trapped in this tangle.
And in all this—love,
which springs from freedom,
as water springs from an oblique rift in the earth.
This is man! He is not transparent,
not monumental,
not simple,
in fact he is poor.

This, one might say, is a more complex view of man than the Ode on the wonder of man in Sophocles' *Antigone*, and the complexity is built into the fabric of the language.

And yet, it is not the verse or the language that gives *The Jeweler's Shop* its rare quality among plays of today, but its dramatic form. Apart from a couple of very short scenes (so short that they scarcely earn the name), the play is composed of monologues spoken by people seemingly together but not talking directly to each other. This is reminiscent of Pinter in his *Landscape* and *Silence* phase, except that, unlike Pinter, Wojtyla's play is not about people's inability to communicate; on the contrary, the monologues of the characters are directly connected, refer to one another, and push the action, such as it is, further on. Such as it is—because it is not a play of external action, but a drama of moral attitudes, of chances taken or lost.

Where did this peculiar dramatic form originate? It is medieval mysteries, Baroque allegories, and more directly the avowed conventions of the Rhapsodic Theater that are the sources from which *The Jeweler's Shop* and the later *Radiation of Fatherhood* trace their dramatic ancestry. During the Nazi occupation of Poland, Karol Wojtyla and his colleagues had to perform in secret to small audiences of some twenty people, in private flats. Of necessity, the visual aspects of the production had to be reduced to a minimum, most often to a single symbolic prop; there was not much scope for movement, so the acting was fairly static.

However, these cramped conditions did not hamper the company's invention or imagination. The arrangement of limited space counted a great deal: the positions that actors occupied, whether left, right, or center, had their meaning, and corresponded somehow to the "mansions" of medieval plays. There was no need for visual effects because the emphasis was on the spoken word, on the *meanings* conveyed by the great texts of the Polish romantics, forbidden by the occupying power. But long narrative poems, such as Juliusz Slowacki's *Beniowski* (1841–44) and *King Spirit* (1846–49), or Adam Mickiewicz's *Pan Tadeusz* (1834), or for that matter the equally long dramas that scarcely lent themselves to conventional stage productions, such as Slowacki's *Samuel Zborowski* (1845), were not recounted in toto. They were carefully arranged into scenarios, extracting the passages most significant and relevant to the audience and performers alike. Thus a kind of "synthesis" of a literary work was presented. The succession of speeches, with actors suggesting rather than "performing" the parts, made for a free and uninterrupted flow of related thoughts.

The Rhapsodic Theater came into the open after the war to continue its activities in a similar style, but though by now certain elements of décor and costume were introduced, the word remained supreme. The theater was twice suppressed by the authorities, first in 1953 during the period of Stalinist repression (it reopened after 1956), then—for good—shortly after its twenty-fifth anniversary, in 1967. In the fifties and early sixties Karol Wojtyla (under his literary pseudonyms Andrzej Jawien and Piotr Jasien) reviewed some of its productions and in so doing restated the Rhapsodic Theater's aims, at the same time throwing light (though not explicitly) on some of his own plays, particularly *The Jeweler's Shop*. In his review of a new production of *King Spirit*, published in the

Krakow *Tygodnik Powszechny* (The Universal Weekly) on January 19, 1958, he wrote:

> This theater, in which there is so much "word" and relatively little "acting," safeguards young actors against the destructive development of individualism, because it will not let them impose on the text anything of their own; it gives the actors an inner discipline . . . A group of people, collectively unanimously somehow subordinated to the great poetic word, prompts reflection on problems of ethics.

Bishop Wojtyla made his purpose clear in a letter to Dr. Kotlarczyk when sending him a copy of *The Jeweler's Shop*: "For quite some time now I have essayed in the 'rhapsodic style,' which seems to me to serve meditation rather than drama (this may be just my own point of view). I am sending you the typescript for perusal." A production of the play by the Rhapsodic Theater was not envisaged. It might possibly be the only kind of theater that could do it successfully, though it has been performed on radio in several countries. In this particular work Jawien-Wojtyla was concerned not so much with constructing an effective "piece of theater" as with "prompting reflection on problems of ethics" through semipoetic, semimoralistic discourse. The dramatic structure of *The Jeweler's Shop*, thanks to the Rhapsodic model the author had in mind, is free from obvious stage conventions, but is nonetheless carefully worked out and lucid. There may be no direct sequence of scenes developing, in linear terms at least, in concrete time and space. There are voices emerging from nowhere, and disappearing into the void after uttering a remark (which usually echoes a character's thoughts); there are snippets of dialogue (really recollections in the minds of the main characters). *The Jeweler's Shop* is, in fact, a drama of inner development, recounted in both the past and the present, as if reflecting a metaphysical perspective. After all, God sees every human life as an entity, not as a moment of time. But it is also a drama presented from the human viewpoint: the Jeweler and his shop are there, or are not there, depending on our need or willingness to perceive them.

The timeless, nonlinear structure of *The Jeweler's Shop*, connected as it is with the author's unique imagery and oblique way of reasoning, makes for complexity. But on another level it is simple enough. The three parts of the play deal with three couples, married or about to be married, loving each other in the present, or having loved each other in the past. Their histories are intertwined—the two central characters in Act III are the children of the couples in the preceding two acts.

The Jeweler stands for the durability of the sacrament of marriage. He not so much sells as dispenses his wedding rings and refuses to take them back when they are no longer wanted, if both the marriage partners are still alive. The mysterious character called Adam, who so strangely enters all the couples' lives, and makes Anna see the Wise Virgins waiting for the Bridegroom, as well as the Foolish Virgins who have lost their chance, is also representative of the providential and guiding forces in life. But, paradoxical though it may seem, the author does not present us with a *drame à thèse*. He writes with insight, and at times with great power, about human love; love that has survived the grave, as in the case of Andrew and Teresa; love that has withered and died, as in the case of

Stefan and Anna; love budding out of complexes, doubts and uncertainties, as in the case of Christopher and Monica. There are no easy solutions, there is no happy ending. But there is hope, if only we can reach out of ourselves, see the true face of the other person, and hear the signals of a Love that transcends us. To this state of mind and heart we are not browbeaten but invited.

The Jeweler's Shop seems to me a significant link between the future Pope John Paul II's writings on ethics (*Love and Responsibility* among them) on the one hand, and his poetry on the other. It combines the elements of a treatise with rich poetic imagery and inner dramatic development. It is the work of a man in whom unbending principles are connected with boundless forbearance and understanding for people. Here, too, out of the chaos created by our human loves, hates and weaknesses, he gently points the way in the right direction.

BOLESLAW TABORSKI

xix

ACT I

❀

THE
SIGNALS

[TERESA AND ANDREW]

1.

TERESA

Andrew has chosen me and asked for my hand.
It happened today between five and six in the afternoon.
I don't remember exactly, I had no time to look at my watch,
or catch a glimpse of the clock on the tower of the old town
        hall.
At such moments one does not check the hour,
such moments grow in one above time.
But even had I remembered to look at the town hall clock,
I could not have done so, for I would have had to
look above Andrew's head.
We were just walking on the right side of the market square
        when Andrew turned around and said,
"Do you want to be my life's companion?"
That's what he said. He didn't say: do you want to be my wife,
but: my life's companion.

What he intended to say must have been thought over.
He said it looking ahead, as if afraid
to read in my eyes, and at the same time as if to signify
that in front of us was a road whose end could not be seen
—there was, or at least, could be,
if I replied "Yes" to his question.

I answered "yes"—not at once,
but after a few minutes,
and yet in the course of those few minutes there was no need
        for reflection,
no need to struggle between motives.
The answer had almost been determined.
We both knew that it reached deep into the past
and advanced far into the future,
that it penetrated our existence like a weaver's shuttle,
to catch the weft that determines a fabric's pattern.

I remember that Andrew did not turn his eyes to me at once,
but looked ahead for quite a while, as if gazing intently
at the road before us.

ANDREW
I went quite a long way before reaching Teresa, I did not find
        her at once.
I do not even remember if our first meeting
was marked by a kind of presentiment.
And I don't think I even know what "love at first sight" means.

4

After a time I realized she had come into the focus of my
     attention,
I mean, I *had to* be interested in her,
and at the same time I *accepted* the fact that I had to.
Though I could have behaved differently from the way I felt I
     must,
I thought there would be no point.
There must have been something in Teresa that suited my
     personality.

I thought much at the time about the "alter ego."
Teresa was a whole world, just as distant
as any other man, as any other woman
—and yet there was something that allowed one to think of
     throwing a bridge.

I let that thought run on, and even develop within me.
It was not an assent independent of an act of will.
I simply resisted sensation and the appeal of the senses,
for I knew that otherwise I would never really leave my "ego"
and reach the other person—but that meant an effort.
For my senses fed at every step
on the charms of the women I met.
When once or twice I tried following them,
I met solitary islands.
This made me think that beauty accessible to the senses
can be a difficult gift or a dangerous one;
I met people led by it to hurt others
—and so, gradually, I learned to value beauty

accessible to the mind, that is to say, truth.
I decided then to seek a woman who would be indeed
my real "alter ego" so that the bridge between us
would not be a shaky footbridge among water lilies and reeds.

I met a few girls who absorbed my imagination,
and also my thoughts—but at the moments
when it seemed to me I was most concerned with them,
I suddenly realized that Teresa was still there in my
        consciousness and memory
and I instinctively compared each of them with her.
And yet I even wished them to push her from my
        consciousness;
in a way, I counted on it.
And I was ready to follow sensation, strong, forceful sensation.

I wanted to regard love as passion,
as an emotion to surpass all
—I believed in the absolute of emotion.
And that is why I could not grasp
the basis of that strange persistence of Teresa in me,
the cause of her presence,
the assurance of her place in my "ego,"
or what creates around her
that strange resonance, that feeling "you ought to."
So I avoided her cautiously, deliberately evaded
everything that could cause even the shadow of a guess.
Sometimes I even tormented her in my thoughts,
while seeing in her my tormentor.
It seemed to me she pursued me with her love,

and that I must cut myself off decisively.
Thus grew my interest in Teresa;
love grew, in a sense, from resistance.
or love can be a collision
in which two selves realize profoundly
they ought to belong to each other, even though they have no
    convenient moods and sensations.
It is one of those processes in the universe which bring a
    synthesis,
unite what was divided, broaden and enrich what was limited
    and narrow.

TERESA

I must admit Andrew's proposal
was something I did not expect.
I really had no reason to count on it.
It always seemed to me that Andrew did everything
to make me useless to him, and to convince me that this was so.

If I was not quite unprepared for his proposal
it was because I felt that somehow I was the right one for him,
and that I supposed I could love him.
Being aware of that, I must already have loved him.
But that was all.
I never allowed myself to nurse a feeling
that remained unanswered.
Today, however, I can admit to myself
that I did not find it easy.

       . . .

7

I recall one month particularly,
and in that month, one evening:
we were hiking in the mountains,
a big group of people but very close,
our friendship was especially strong—
we understood one another perfectly.
Andrew was then quite clearly interested in Christine.
But this did not spoil the pleasure of the ramble for me.
For I was always as hard as a tree
that would rather rot than topple.
If I cried for myself,
it was not from disappointed love.
And yet it was difficult.

That evening, particularly, night fell as we were going down,
and I shall never forget the small lakes that surprised us on
            the way
like two cisterns of unfathomable sleep.
There was metal asleep, mixed with the reflection
of a bright August night.
And yet there was no moon.

Suddenly, as we were standing and watching
—I shan't forget this as long as I live—
somewhere above our heads
we clearly heard a call.
It was rather like
wailing or like a groan,
or even a whine maybe.

.   .   .

Everyone held his breath.
It was not clear whether it was a man calling,
or a late bird wailing.
The same call was repeated once more,
and then the boys decided to call back.
Through the quiet sleeping woods,
through the mountain night* went a signal.
If it was a man—he would hear it.
The first voice, however, was heard no more.

And just then, when everyone had grown silent,
listening in case the call might ring out once more,
I was suddenly struck by another thought: also about signals;
that thought returned to me today
between Andrew's profile
and the tower of the old town hall
in our city—
today between five and six in the afternoon,
when Andrew asked me for my hand—

then I was thinking about signals that could not connect.
It was a thought about Andrew and myself.
And I felt how difficult it is to live.
That night was terribly hard for me,
though it was a truly glorious mountain* night,
and full of nature's secrets.
Everything around seemed

* In the original, *noc bieszczadzka*—"Bieszczady night," referring to
the Bieszczady range of mountains in southeastern Poland.—B.T.

so very necessary
and so in harmony with the world's totality,
only man was off balance and lost.
Perhaps not every human being,
but I know for certain that I was.
So today, when Andrew asked,
"Would you like to become forever my life's companion?,"
after ten minutes I answered "Yes,"
and after a while I asked him if he believed in signals.

ANDREW

Teresa asked me today:
"Andrew, do you believe in signals?"
And when I, surprised at this question,
stopped for a moment
and looked, astonished, into my fiancée's eyes—
my fiancée of a quarter of an hour—
she told me her thoughts,
those that had been revolving in her head
since the evening in the mountains.

How close she passed by me then;
she almost hemmed me in with her imagination
and that discreet suffering,
which at the time I did not want to know,
and today am willing to regard as our common good.

Teresa—Teresa—Teresa—
like a strange focus of my way to maturity—

no longer a prism of superficial rays,
but a being of true light.
And I know I cannot go further.
I know I shall not seek anymore.
I only tremble at the thought that
I could so easily have lost her.

For several years she had been walking by me, and I did not
   know
that it was she who was walking and maturing.
I recoiled from accepting
what today is for me a most magnificent gift.
Several years later I see it clearly
that roads which should have diverged
have brought us closer together.
Those years have been invaluable, giving us time
to get our bearings on the complicated
map of signs and signals.

It must be so.
Today I see that my country is also her country,
and, after all, I dreamed of throwing a bridge—

2.

In the evenings, in our old city
(evenings in October begin early)
men leave their offices,
where new housing developments are planned,

women and girls on the way home
look in shop windows.

I met Teresa when she had just paused
in front of a large window
full of ladies' shoes.
I stopped by her quietly and unexpectedly
—and suddenly we were together
on both sides of the big transparent sheet
filled with glowing light.
And we saw our reflections together,
because behind the window display
is a great, immense mirror,
which reflects the shoe models
as well as the people passing on the pavement,
particularly those who have stopped
to look at themselves, or at the shoes.

So when we found ourselves all of a sudden
on both sides of the great mirror
—here alive and real, there reflected—
I—who knows why,
maybe to complete the picture,
but more likely just in answer to my heart's need—
asked, "What are you thinking about, Teresa?"
I asked this almost in a whisper,
for this is how those in love are wont to talk.

I wasn't thinking then about signals anymore.
And I wasn't really thinking about Andrew.
I was looking for high-heeled shoes.
There were many sports shoes,
many comfortable walking shoes,
but I was really straining my eyes
for high-heeled shoes.

Andrew is so much taller than I
that I have to add a little to my height
—and so I was thinking about Andrew,
about Andrew and about myself.
I was now constantly thinking about us two;
he must surely think like this too—
so he must rejoice at my thought.

We then began to talk
about all sorts of little things connected with our wedding.
I told him about the tie
in which I like him most,
and about the dark suit
which best becomes him.
Andrew listened to all this gladly,
not because he wished to be flattered,
but because he wanted me always to find him attractive,
and wanted to please me.

Then we looked together
in the window of a jeweler's shop,

where in little boxes,
inlaid with velvet,
jewelry was exhibited.
Among them were wedding rings.
We looked for a while in silence.
Then Andrew took me by the hand
and said, "Let's go in, Teresa;
we'll choose our rings."

ANDREW

And yet we did not go in at once,
held back by a thought which
—we felt this clearly—arose at the same time
in me and in her.

The rings in the window
appealed to us with a strange force.
Now they are just artifacts of precious metal,
but it will be so only until that moment
when I put one of them on Teresa's finger,
and she puts the other on mine.
From then on they will mark our fate.
They will constantly act as a reminder of the past,
as a lesson to be memorized for good,
and they will constantly open up the future,
joining the past to the future.
By the same token, they are, for all time,
like two last links in a chain,
to unite us invisibly.

. . .

So we did not enter the shop at once. The symbol spoke.
We both understood it immediately. Looking at wedding
     rings,
we yielded to emotion, without words.
That was what held us up in front of the shop. We put off the
     moment of entry.
I only felt Teresa cling more tightly
to my shoulder . . . and that was our "now":
the meeting of the past with the future.
Here we both are, we grow out of so many strange moments,
as if from the depths of facts, ordinary and simple though
     they are.
Here we are together. We are secretly growing into one
because of these two rings.

Someone spoke quite loudly behind our backs.

SOMEONE

This is the jeweler's shop. What a strange craft.
To produce objects that can
stimulate reflection on fate.
To gild watches, for instance, which measure time
and tell man about the transience of all things
and their passing.

TERESA

Someone ceased to speak. The man found his way, however,
to the edge of our thoughts. We went on standing in silence.

. . .

Imagination worked, though. I already saw, as in a mirror,
myself, in a white wedding dress, kneeling with Andrew,
dressed in a black suit. As we entered the church
I equaled him in height, inasmuch as there was no
        disproportion
(this was why I had to buy the high-heeled shoes
I saw today in that other window).

And now—the strangest thing
and unexpected:
as we were standing thus in front of the jeweler's
we remembered fragments of letters
written a few years ago.

3.

[*Fragments of Teresa's letter to Andrew*]
. . . I want to return, Andrew, to our August hike, to that
night when we heard those strange signals. You remember,
there was some confusion and difference of opinion. Some
thought that we ought to begin a search for wanderers who
might be lost in the thick of the forest, while some, on the
other hand, took the view that it had been a late bird calling,
not a man. You were among the latter.
    It was a memorable night, also memorable because it was
then—it seems to me, Andrew—that I saw you in truth. And
believe me, the contrasts dormant in you almost struck me in
the face. A disproportion between the wish for happiness and
a man's potential is unavoidable. But you try to calculate your

happiness at any price, just as you calculate everything in your planning office. You lack courage and trust—in what? in whom? in life, in your own fate, in people, in God . . .

[*Fragments of Andrew's letter to Teresa*]
. . . so you are courageous and full of trust—and yet how many times did I see tears in your face, though your eyes remained dry. Maybe you think you courageously reach for happiness, but in fact this is only another form of fear—or caution at least.

4.

TERESA

Imagination was working more and more intensely,
ranging over reminiscences, over the past,
to the future, whose picture was ever nearer.
So, I see myself near Andrew, equal to him in height.
We are both elegant and somehow mature
—we matured through so many letters exchanged during
those years.
We are still standing in front of that shop, choosing our fate
together.
But the window has turned into a mirror of our future
—it reflects its shape.

The wedding rings did not stay in the window.
The jeweler looked long into our eyes.
Testing for the last time the fineness of precious metal,
he spoke seriously, deep thoughts,
which remained strangely in my memory.

"The weight of these golden rings,"
he said, "is not the weight of metal,
but the proper weight of man,
each of you separately
and both together.
Ah, man's own weight,
the proper weight of man!
Can it be at once heavier,
and more intangible?
It is the weight of constant gravity,
riveted to a short flight.
The flight has the shape of a spiral, an ellipse—and the shape
        of the heart . . .
Ah, the proper weight of man!
This rift, this tangle, this ultimate depth—
this clinging, when it is so hard
to unstick heart and thought.
And in all this—freedom,
a freedom, and sometimes frenzy,
the frenzy of freedom trapped in this tangle.
And in all this—love,
which springs from freedom,
as water springs from an oblique rift in the earth.

This is man! He is not transparent,
not monumental,
not simple,
in fact he is poor.
This is one man—and what about two people,
four, a hundred, a million—
multiply all this
(multiply the greatness by the weakness),
and you will have the product of humanity,
the product of human life."

This is what the strange jeweler was saying
while taking the measure of our rings.
Then he cleaned them with chamois leather,
and put them back in the little box,
which had earlier been in the window,
and finally wrapped it in tissue paper.
All this while he looked into our eyes,
as if he wished to sound our hearts.
Was he right in saying all that?
Were his thoughts also ours?
I suppose neither of us could
think about it from such a distance—
love is enthusiasm rather than pensiveness.

TERESA

So, we are standing reflected in the window,
as if in a mirror that catches the future:
Andrew takes one of the rings,

I take the other, we take each other by the hand—
my God, how simple this is.

What can the people think invited to our wedding?
What do they think when they are silent—
and what will they go on thinking when they stop talking?

5.

CHORUS

1. The occasion is most beautiful,
   it evokes so many associations.
   We are looking only at what is!
           2. Man lives with a shadow line,
              he lives also with a line of light.
              The light passes into shadow,
              shadow into light.
3. New people—Teresa and Andrew—
   two until now, but still not one,
   one from now on, though still two.
           4. She seems sad, though,
              but perhaps she's just serious
              and moved—
              (a diamond flashed on Andrew's shirt
                 front,
              a white flower in Teresa's hair,
              though it's a different flash).
5. Wine also sparkles. Wine is a thing.
   Let it live in the other man,

man—is love. Teresa and Andrew
wine, wine—
radiate mutually into each other's lives.
(Raise your glass.)

6. Ah, how many words and hearts
ah, how many words and hearts
ah, how many words and hearts

And we'll go on with you along the
cloister
we'll go then down the avenue,
a few score, a few hundred yards,
with enthusiasm,
with a sincere smile,
up to now, up to now together.
Later vehicles will appear,
later a road will hinder us
—when you get into the car
you must stay alone.

7. But let us return to the stars,
let us return to warmth, to feelings.
Ah, how man thirsts for feelings,
how people thirst for intimacy.
Teresa and Andrew.

8. Trees, trees—straight, slender trunks,
cutting high, high above the eyes
cutting the moon distant from the eyes
three hundred thousand miles—
and yet they are two.
Teresa and Andrew.

The moon becomes a little drum
that plays in the depths of eyes
and in the depths of hearts.

9. Love—love pulsating in brows,
in man becomes thought
and will:
the will of Teresa being Andrew,
the will of Andrew being Teresa.

      10. Strange, yet necessary
         —and again we move away from each
         other
      because man will not endure in
         man forever
      and man will not suffice.

11. How can it be done, Teresa,
for you to stay in Andrew forever?
How can it be done, Andrew,
for you to stay in Teresa forever?
Since man will not endure in man
and man will not suffice.

      12. Body—thought passes through it,
         is not satisfied in the body—
         and love passes through it.
         Teresa, Andrew, seek
         a harbor for thought in your bodies
         while they last,
         seek the harbor for love.

Though we were still standing in front of the jeweler's shop
. . . it was nonetheless clear that his shop window had ceased
to be a display in which everyone without exception could find
an object for himself. It became, however, a mirror reflecting
us both—Teresa and myself. Moreover, it was not an ordinary
flat mirror, but a lens absorbing its object. We were not only
reflected but absorbed. I had an impression of being seen and
recognized by someone hiding inside the shop window.

TERESA

One could see in it our wedding day. We were both dressed
in our Sunday best, and behind us there were a lot of people:
they were wedding guests. The window absorbed my person
at various moments and in different situations—first as I was
standing, then kneeling by Andrew, when we were exchanging
the rings . . . I am also convinced that our reflection in that
mirror has remained forever, and cannot be extracted or removed. A little while later we concluded that we had been
present in the mirror from the beginning—at any rate much
sooner than the moment we stopped in front of the jeweler's
shop.

ANDREW

And the jeweler, as I have already mentioned, looked at us in
a peculiar way. His gaze was at once gentle and penetrating.
I had a feeling he was watching us while he was selecting and
weighing the rings. He then put them on our fingers to try

them. I had the feeling that he was seeking our hearts with his eyes and delving into our past. Does he encompass the future too? The expression of his eyes combined warmth with determination. The future for us remains an unknown quantity, which we now accept without anxiety. Love has overcome anxiety. The future depends on love.

TERESA

The future depends on love.

ANDREW

At one point my eyes once more met the gaze of the old jeweler. I felt just then that His gaze was not only sounding our hearts, but also trying to impart something to us. We found ourselves not only on the level of His gaze, but also on the level of His life. Our whole existence stood before Him. His eyes were flashing signals which we were not able to receive fully just then, as once we had been unable to receive fully the signals in the mountains—and yet, they reached to our inner hearts. And somehow we went in their direction, and they covered the fabric of our whole lives.

TERESA

We stood in front of the jeweler's shop for a long time, without noticing the time, or the cold of the October evening. At one point, though, we were roused by these words, spoken loudly by a passer-by behind our backs:

SOMEONE

It is late and the shops are closed. Why is the light still on in the old jeweler's workshop? He too should lock up and go home.

ACT II

❀

THE BRIDEGROOM

[ANNA AND STEFAN]

1.

Looking back over the events of recent days,
I must have been in quite a state.
I must have looked with bitterness.
Bitterness is a taste of food and drink,
it is also an inner taste—a taste of the soul
when it has suffered disappointment or disillusionment.
That taste permeates everything we happen
to say, think or do; it permeates even our smile.

Did I really suffer disappointment and disillusionment?
Could it be merely the ordinary course of things
determined by the history of two people?
This is precisely how Stefan attempts to explain it,
since I confessed to him at once
the first grievance that arose in me.
Stefan listened, but I did not have the impression
that he took to heart what I told him.

My grievance grew because of that.
He does not love me anymore—I must have thought—
since he does not react to my grief.

I could not reconcile myself to this,
nor could I prevent
a rift opening between us
(its edges stood still at first,
but at any moment they could move apart
wider and wider—
at any rate, I did not feel them
moving closer together again).
It was as if Stefan had ceased to be in me.
Did I cease to be in him too?
Or was it simply that I felt
I now existed only in myself?
At first I felt such a stranger
in myself!
It was as if I had become unaccustomed to the walls of my
        interior—
so full had they been of Stefan
that without him they seemed empty.
Is it not too terrible a thing
to have committed the walls of my interior
to a single inhabitant
who could disinherit my self
and somehow deprive me of my place in it!

Outwardly nothing changed.
Stefan seemed to behave the same,

                    .   .   .

but he could not heal the wound
that had opened in my soul.
It did not hurt him, he did not feel it.
Maybe he did not want to. Will it heal of itself?
But if it heals of itself,
it will still somehow separate us.
Meanwhile, Stefan was sure
he did not have anything to heal.
He left me with a hidden wound,
thinking, no doubt, She will get over it.
Besides, he was confident of his rights,
whereas I wanted him to win them continually.
I did not want to feel like an object
that cannot be lost
once it has been acquired.
Was there a kind of selfishness in all this?
—I certainly did not do enough
to justify Stefan to myself.
After all, is love to be a compromise?
Should it not be born continuously out of a struggle
for the love of another human being?

So I fought for Stefan's love,
ready to retreat at any time
if he did not realize the sense
of the battle.

In the end, however, shall I forgive?
Or is the rift to be permanent?
It is very hard, this borderline
between selfishness and unselfishness.

I was a mother. Every night
our children went to sleep in the next room:
Mark, who was the eldest, Monica and John.
There was silence in the nursery:
—that rift in our love,
which I felt so painfully,
had not yet passed into the souls of the children.

2.

A CHANCE INTERLOCUTOR

I saw that woman here for the second time.
She was passing by the old jeweler's shop.
The shutters were already lowered, the door padlocked.
The jeweler finishes his work at seven
and leaves.
Working all day long, he may not realize
how deeply his craft penetrates a man's life.
I talked to him once about that.
The shop's door was open and the jeweler was standing on the
        threshold,
watching the passers-by, casually it seemed.
The sun was shining, so the street was full of brightness,
making people blink.
Men and women were putting on their dark glasses
to avoid being dazzled by the blaze.
Through dark spectacles you do not see the color of eyes,
which sink in the dark as if in a well.
And yet from behind such glasses

you see everything (though peculiarly tinted),
without blinking.

The jeweler's shop is now closed.
The faces of passers-by hide in the evening dusk.

ANNA

I have often walked past here.
It was on my way home every day after work
(on the way to work I take shortcuts).
In the past I paid no attention
to this shop.
But since
the rift in our love became a fact,
I have often looked at golden wedding rings
—the symbols of human love and "marital faith."
I remember the past appeal of that symbol
when love was something indisputable,
a melody played on all
the strings of the heart.
Later the strings became gradually muted
and neither of us could do anything about it.
I thought that the guilt was Stefan's—
and could find no guilt in myself.
Life changed
into a more and more strenuous existence of two people
who occupied
less and less room in each other.
Only the sum of duties remained,

a sum total conventional and changing,
removed further and further away
from the pure taste of enthusiasm.
And so little, so little, joins together.

I thought then about the wedding rings,
which we both, Stefan and I,
wore on our fingers.
One day, on the way back from work,
passing by the jeweler's shop,
I thought I might as well
sell this ring of mine.
(Stefan probably would not have noticed—
I had almost ceased to exist for him.
Whether he was unfaithful to me I do not know,
since I took no interest in his life either.
He was indifferent to me.
I suppose after office hours he went to play cards,
and after drinking he would come home quite late,
without saying a word, or with some casual remark,
to which as a rule I responded with silence.)
So this time I decided to go in.

The jeweler examined the workmanship, weighed the ring
for a long time in his fingers and looked
into my eyes. For a while he was reading
the date of our wedding
engraved inside the ring.
Again he looked into my eyes, put the ring on the scales . . .
then said, "This ring does not weigh anything,
the needle does not move from zero

and I cannot make it show
even a milligram.
Your husband must be alive—
in which case neither of your rings, taken separately,
will weigh anything—only both together will register.
My jeweler's scales
have this peculiarity
that they weigh not the metal
but man's entire being and fate."
Ashamed, I took the ring back
and left the shop without a word
—I think, though, that he followed me with his eyes.

Since that day I have taken a different route back home.
Only again today . . . but I found the shop closed.

A CHANCE INTERLOCUTOR

The woman whom I met by the jeweler's shop
was not there by chance—
of this I am absolutely certain.
I think, however, that it was by chance
that I started a conversation with her
as a result of which
she revealed her life to me.
She complained in the end that the old jeweler
did not want to buy the ring which she no longer needed.

In the course of that conversation I could see
the whole span of human love
and its precipitous edges.

When someone slips over such an edge
he finds it very hard to get back,
and wanders alone below the road he should be on.

About Stefan I learned from Anna's words as much,
as if I were to be his judge and the executor of the verdict.
But the jeweler was not there,
and no one to confirm these words.

ANNA

I was surprised at myself
for having begun such a conversation
with a total stranger.
I told him about Stefan and myself,
making use of the fact that he was listening
and did not interrupt my flow of words.
It was a monologue, really,
prepared in great detail in my mind.
Fact followed fact, charges against Stefan.
I was sure of the truth of my judgments.
But I also talked like a woman
about the inner crack in love,
about the rift, and the wound which hurts . . .

The man listened to me with concentration.
I did not know his Christian name or even his surname.
He did not ask me mine, either.
And yet at a certain moment
he said, "Anna" (so he did mention my name)

36

"how very like me you are
—you, and Stefan too,
you are both like me.
And my name is Adam."

I wanted to ask for his address
(I thought of writing a few words to him one day).
Then we were walking for a while down the street.
I felt so well
in the company of that man.
I was struck by his appearance,
so manly and so grave.
Thought dominated, and a tinge of pain
(how different he is from Stefan).

Adam said all of a sudden,
when after a while we paused at the same place,
"Here is the jeweler's shop again;
soon the Bridegroom will pass by."

ADAM

Then I told that woman (Anna):
"The Bridegroom will come shortly . . ."
I said this, thinking of the love
which had so died in her soul.
The Bridegroom passes through so many streets,
meeting so many different people.
Passing, he touches the love
that is in them. If it is bad,

he suffers for it. Love is bad
when there is a lack of it.

I remember—I also asked that woman,
"Why do you wish to sell your ring here?
What do you want to break with this gesture—your life?
Does one not sell one's life now and again?
Does one not break one's entire life
with every gesture?
But what of it? The thing is not to go away,
and wander for days, months, even years—
the thing is to return and in the old place
to find oneself. Life is an adventure,
and at the same time it has its logic
and consistency—
that is why one must not leave thought
and imagination on their own!"
"With what is thought to remain, then?" Anna asked.
It is to remain with truth, of course.

                    ANNA
Isn't what one feels most strongly the truth?

Our conversation took an unexpected turn—
so I was not sure where else it could lead.
This was the fruit of my sensitivity and his intelligence.

Stefan left my awareness for a while,
and yet I felt then, too, how unable I was

to forgive him for having disgraced my reflection in him,
my being which somehow must have existed in him
—after all, I was his wife . . .
I was delicate no less than passionate—
is not love a matter of the senses and of a climate
which unites and makes two people walk
in the sphere of their feeling?—this is the whole truth.

Adam, however, did not fully agree with this.
Love is, according to him, a synthesis of two people's
          existence
which converges, as it were, at a certain point.
and makes them into one.

And then again he repeated
that the Bridegroom would walk down this street
shortly.
This news, heard for the second time,
not only fascinated me
but suddenly awoke a longing in me.
A longing for someone perfect,
for a man firm and good,
who would be different from Stefan,
different, different . . .
And with the feeling of this sudden longing
I felt different and younger myself.
I must even have started running,
looking closely at the men I was passing—

. . . The first of them did not even look in my direction when I brushed past him. He walked, clearly lost in thought. He may have been thinking about his business. Perhaps he was the manager of a firm, or the chief accountant of some big concern. Without even turning his head he just said "Sorry."

I

Sorry.

ANNA

I did not try to stop him; I was, however, ready to attract his attention. I don't know how it was that I then felt ready to try and make every man notice me. It might have been just a simple reflection of that longing, but I was convinced that no one could take that right from me.

ADAM

This is just what compels me to think about human love. There is no other matter embedded more strongly in the surface of human life, and there is no matter more unknown and more mysterious. The divergence between what lies on the surface and the mystery of love constitutes precisely the source of the drama. It is one of the greatest dramas of human existence. The surface of love has its current—swift, flickering, changeable. A kaleidoscope of waves and situations full of attraction. This current is sometimes so stunning that it carries people away—women and men. They got carried away by the thought that they have absorbed the whole secret of love, but in fact they have not yet even touched it. They are happy for a while, thinking they have reached the limits of existence and wrested all its secrets from it, so that nothing remains. That's how it is: on the other side of that rapture nothing remains, there is nothing left behind it. But there can't be nothing, there can't! Listen to me, there can't. Man is a *continuum*, a totality and a continuity—so it cannot be that nothing remains!

ANNA

The second passer-by I met reacted differently. When I looked him in the face, he noticed my look and stopped. He returned the look, walked two steps toward me and said, "I must have seen you somewhere before . . ."

II

. . . I must have seen you somewhere before . . .

ANNA

I was almost ready to cling to his arm. It was such a warm evening, and so many lights filtered through the rusting October leaves. One could not see the rust at night, of course. I longed so much for a man's arm and a walk along the avenue of wilting chestnut trees. He went on to say, "How about stepping into that club . . . A little light music would do you good . . ."

III

. . . How about stepping into that club . . . A little light music would do you good . . .

ANNA

"And then?" He did not reply, and I seemed to take fright at that "then." He must have had a wife, about whom he wouldn't say anything just then. Suddenly I realized what the expression "a casual woman" could mean. And something made me not cling to his arm. He was not too insistent, though. And I understood even more clearly what the expression "a casual woman" might mean.

I don't know how many steps I took or in what direction. I must have walked from the avenue surrounding the old part of town toward that church in whose recesses stand the statues of the saints. In a niche at the back—I remember—is a crucifix, in front of which a lamp burns at night. I seemed to see its light already, dimmed by the multicolored glass of the lantern.

I kept walking, however, still thinking about the same thing, coming forward, as it were, toward every passing man. One passed by so fast, and so close, that he caught the end of his briefcase in the rib of my umbrella hanging from my right arm. Another took his hat off, looked intently at my face, and quickly put his hat on again; I heard him mumble something like "No, I don't know her"—and he walked away.

IV

... No ... I don't know her ...

ANNA

Now I'm on the edge of the pavement. On the curb. I am walking along the curb, as I used to when I was a little girl. I could then run on the curb along the street and my foot never slipped off into the road. This was a favorite game with my friends; we used to boast: "I ran all along Cool Street and Prus Street and fell off only once"; "I never fell off—you see who's better ..."

Now I am walking on the curb again, I am not running. My eyes are dry but I know they are shining. There's a car; an expensive one. The window is partly lowered, a man at the wheel. I stopped.

ADAM

Love is not an adventure. It has the taste of the whole man. It has his weight. And the weight of his whole fate. It cannot be a single moment. Man's eternity passes through it. That is why it is to be found in the dimensions of God, because only He is eternity.

Man looking out into time. To forget, to forget. To be for a moment only, only now—and cut oneself off from eternity. To take in everything at one moment and lose everything immediately after. Ah, the curse of that next moment and all the moments that follow, moments through which you will look for the way back to the moment that has passed, to have it once more, and through it—everything.

ANNA

I stopped and fixed my eyes on the car, the windows, the man. I remember how Stefan used to say, "One day, darling, I'll buy a car; we'll drive into the unknown, we beautiful and elegant people." The man looked. I approached. He lowered the window even more. He had a low, warm voice when he said, "Won't you join me?"

V

. . . Won't you join me?

ANNA

He indicated the seat next to him. In a while, he will start the engine. We shall move off. We'll drive into the unknown. A man's hands on the wheel. One could lean slightly against his arm as he unfolds the ribbon of the road. Then the lights from above . . . I shall be somebody again. He repeated the words once more.

44

VI

... Won't you join me...?

I want to, I think I want to very much.

I think I had already put my hand on the door handle. I only had to press it. Suddenly I felt a man's hand on mine. I looked up. Adam was standing above me. I saw his face, which was tired; it betrayed emotion. Adam looked me straight in the eyes. He did not say anything. His hand was just lying on mine. Then he said "No."

No.

I felt the car moving past us. In a moment it was gone. Adam let go of my hand. I must have said, "It's strange that you should come back; I thought you'd disappeared for good. Where were you all this time?"

I came back to show you the street. It is strange. Not because it is full of shops, neon lights and buildings, but because of the people. Look, on the other side of the street there are some girls passing by; they are walking, laughing and talking loudly among themselves. Ah, I don't suppose you know where they are going.

Their lamps are out, so they are on their way to buy some oil. They will fill the lamps, and the lamps will burn again.

ANNA

Oh yes . . .

ADAM

They are the wise virgins. Count them. There ought to be five. They've gone past. You're wondering why they are not wearing long oriental robes. They are dressed according to the climate and customs of our country. But they are carrying lanterns and people are surprised, wondering where they are taking them. Or maybe they are not surprised, for nowadays people are not usually surprised by anything.

And now look over there. Those are the foolish virgins. They are asleep and their lamps are lying by the wall. One has even rolled across the pavement and fallen into the gutter.

To you it seems that they are asleep in those recesses, but in reality they too are walking down the street. They are walking in their sleep. They are walking in a lethargy—they have a dormant space in them. You now feel that space in you, because you too were falling asleep. I have come to wake you. I think I am in time.

46

ANNA

Why did you wake me? Why?

ADAM

I've wakened you because the Bridegroom is to walk down this street. The wise virgins want to come forward and meet him with their lights; the foolish virgins have fallen asleep and lost their lamps. I promise you they will not wake in time, and even if they do, they will not be able to find and light their lamps.

ANNA

Indeed—the lamps have rolled across the street, and if you are suddenly awakened, for a while you are still full of sleep. But the Bridegroom will pass by quickly. He is sure to be a young man and will not wait.

ADAM

Well, he is constantly waiting. He continually lives in expectation. Only this is, as it were, on the far side of all those different loves without which man cannot live. Take you, for instance. You cannot live without love. I saw from a distance how you walked down this street and tried to rouse interest. I could almost hear your soul. You were calling with despair for a love you do not have. You were looking for someone who would take you by the hand and hug you.

Ah, Anna, how am I to prove to you that on the other side of all those loves which fill our lives—there is *Love!* The Bridegroom is coming down this street and walks every street! How am I to prove to you that you are the bride? One would now have to pierce a layer of your soul, as one pierces the layer of brushwood and soil when looking for a source of water in the green of a wood. You would then hear him speak: beloved, you do not know how deeply you are mine, how much you belong to my love and my suffering—because to love means to give life through death; to love means to let gush a spring of the water of life into the depths of the soul, which burns or smolders, and cannot burn out. Ah, the flame and the spring. You don't feel the spring but are consumed by the flame. Is that not so?

ANNA

I don't know. I only know you have been talking to my soul. Don't be afraid. It goes with my body. How can it be embraced or possessed without my body? I am a foolish virgin. I am one of the foolish virgins. Why did you wake me?

ADAM

The Bridegroom is coming. This is his precise hour. Oh, look—the wise virgins have just gone by, holding their freshly lighted lamps. Their light is bright, because they have cleaned the glass in the lanterns. They walk gaily, almost dancing as they walk.

There they are again, those girls. Their faces are not even attentive. Are they really pure and noble, or is it just that they have fared better in life than I?

O foolish, foolish woman, wakened to go on sleeping—

Then I went on looking. A man was walking, dressed in a light coat, he was not wearing a hat. I did not notice his face at first, because he walked lost in thought, his head lowered. On impulse I began to walk in his direction. But when he lifted his face, I nearly gave a shout. It seemed to me I clearly saw Stefan's face. And I immediately withdrew toward where Adam was standing. I grasped him firmly by the hand. Adam was saying:

ADAM

I know why you have turned back. You could not stand the sight of his face.

ANNA

I have seen the face I hate, and the face I ought to love. Why do you expose me to such a test?

ADAM

In the Bridegroom's face each of us finds a similarity to the faces of those with whom love has entangled us on this side of life, of existence. They are all in him.

49

ANNA

I am afraid.

ADAM

You are afraid of love. Are you really afraid of love?

ANNA

Yes. I am afraid. Well, why do you torment me? That man had Stefan's face. I am afraid of that face.

4.

CHORUS, STEFAN

1. Lights have paused, words have paused,
   no pause for the thoughts or the drama.
   People remain the same.
   Fate separates them,
   makes them change,
   forming no unity.
2. The lamps burn low on the pavement
   —has their oil burned out?
   It is not with oil that the flame is fed,
   but with rain water—
   the pavement and the roadway are wet in the falling rain.
3. Foolish virgins, O foolish virgins,
   no one can strike a flame from water!

(Human feet are protected from the wet
by shoes.)
4. Let illusion and fiction be gone:
no one has passed by, the light has not been taken away.
Everything remains as it was.
The green is fed by rain
—the trees have not yet rusted.
Anna's wet hair and Stefan's arm
and coat—
5. This has been. No one allows it to return.
Wet hair, because it's spring or autumn. Do not cry!
You are not free, you are not different
—only the rain falls obliquely.
6. And the wicks drink oil,
and the water drinks flame,
and the stone does not drink water
—doesn't drink—doesn't drink—
but the water has drunk the flame
and the lamps are out.
7. Two lamps are out.
One didn't give its flame to the other.
One didn't give oil to the other.
Didn't give its wick.

Didn't give its wick,
didn't give
—two lamps—and the rain.
8. The night is falling and he has brought light.
Has brought it and taken it away.

And wanted to become you and me,
him and her.
But he has gone.
Who knows what time it is now?
9. It is I. It is I. Stefan's arm is weak
and Anna's hair has dried. And her eyes . . .

5.

ANNA

When I roused myself from my visions and meditations,
I was still standing in the same place.
The jeweler's shop was shut as before.

I recall the expression of his eyes,
which independently of his words uttered this command:
"You must never be below the level of my sight;
you must not fall lower, for the weight of your life
must be shown on my scales."

When I then ran, so full of hidden hope,
toward the Bridegroom so suddenly promised,
I saw Stefan's face.
Must he have that face for me?
Why? Why?

ACT III

❀

THE CHILDREN

[MONICA AND CHRISTOPHER]

1.

The day Christopher told me about Monica
I walked back home more slowly than ever before,
as if deliberately looking for new streets and roundabout
     routes.
After all, I had to ponder my son's words
and seek a climate for them in my own heart.

I had known of her before. She was one
of Christopher's fellow students. I also knew
that Christopher was interested in the girl.
I saw her a few times—she was a shy and delicate
child. Made on me the impression
of a being enclosed in herself, whose true value
gravitates inward so much that it simply ceases
to reach other people. Is that a true value?

. . .

So I thought about Monica among unknown streets,
but I kept seeing Christopher. Thinking about him
had become something as close to me as my own existence.
It had bored so many paths through my consciousness
that wherever a thought began,
it was bound to come across one of them.

Just now I am (I suppose) in front of the jeweler's shop.
And all of a sudden I can see something like a mirror,
where the fates of Andrew and myself were once reflected.
We stood for a long time on the threshold. It was an October
        evening.
The wedding rings were lying before us in the window.
Then we saw them on the fingers of our hands.
Our nearest future was there in that strange mirror.
Well-wishing people entered through the wall of that vision,
we heard their conversations—even more: their thoughts.
And we both, Andrew and I, with the help of two gold rings,
became one—
    To that point only we read in the mirror;
the rest is unknown.

Christopher was not yet born, though conceived in me.
And Andrew's later fate, the history of our union,
everything then unknown, was now made flesh.
When Christopher was two years old, Andrew went to the
        front.
He took the child and hugged him for a long time before the
        door closed behind him.

That was the last vision—and Christopher does not know his
        father.
Our union remained in that child, nothing more.
Christopher grew up,
Andrew did not die in me, did not die on any front,
he did not even have to come back, for somehow he is.

You have no notion, my husband, how terrible the fear is
that borders on hope and penetrates it daily.
There is no hope without fear, and no fear without hope.
And Christopher grew—and more and more I saw you in him.
So I did not leave the sphere of your most strange person,
to whom I had given myself, from whom I do not know how
        to withdraw.
You do not come, do not even take the trouble.
On the far side of the mirror the jeweler fitted the rings.
On the far side of the mirror our fate was split
—but the union remained.

Christopher, Christopher told me today about Monica,
the strange, shy girl—
just as you once said to your mother: "Teresa."
The word has been uttered.

So I stood today again in front of the jeweler's shop,
reading the continuation of our strange story.
That old man had in his eyes the plane of our new existence.
Our hearts were the vertical. (The vertical and the plane
        met.)

.   .   .

57

Then I saw them together—they were leaving, both joyful.
Monica in her smile betrayed a discreet breakthrough:
Christopher had read the person, and their thought suffused
    each other.
(For a moment I felt that I was Monica to be met again by
    you.)
They could have passed by, not noticed me even—
and yet all their conversation had to be contained in me.

2.

[*Such was the conversation of Christopher and Monica*]

CHRISTOPHER

I am my mother's child and find her in you too.
I do not remember my father—so I don't know what a man
    ought to be.
I am beginning my life anew. I lack ready models.
Father remained in Mother, when he fell somewhere at the
    front,
and did not visit me anymore, was not with me day by day.
Mother implanted the idea of Father in me—thus I grew up,
thinking more often than you imagine about her woman's fate,
about her loneliness full of the absent man,
whom I embody with my presence . . .
But I do not want this fate for you. I want the presence,
in the future the suffusion we have now.
Is there so much of my mother in you that I have to leave her
to find her in you? This life is altogether new,

and people are new: thank you for precisely this—
that you have compelled me, Monica, to grasp my existence
as an untold completenesss, enhanced
and delineated because you have drawn near.

M O N I C A

And yet I am afraid of myself, and also afraid for you.
Before that, for a long time I was afraid of you, and for
     myself.
Your father went away and died, and yet the union remained
—you were its spokesman, the love passed to you.
My parents live like two strangers,
the union one dreams of does not exist,
where one person wants to accept, and to give, life for two.
Will it not be a mistake, my dear, will it not come to an end?
One day will you not leave as my father has,
who is a stranger at home; shall I not leave, like Mother,
who has become a stranger? Is human love at all
capable of enduring through man's whole existence?
Well, what pervades me now is the feeling of love
—but I am also pervaded by a feeling of the future,
and that is fear.

I know—you took it from me (that is how love began),
you took it once in your hands, like a second pair of hands
frozen cold and in danger of never getting warm
—these were my hands . . . remember, Christopher, skiing
at the edge of that forest, with the sun setting fast,
and we had lost the way. I was also afraid of you,

59

of that strength of yours, which could master me,
then leave me . . . (that was a feeling for the future).
Now I am more afraid of myself, having gained confidence
      in you.
You said that your father had gone and never returned,
and yet he has remained, Christopher—not like my father,
and not like my mother. So I thought to myself once
that you too would remain, even if you went like your father—
And everything has changed since then. I began to be afraid
      for you.

CHRISTOPHER

We have to accept the fact that love weaves itself into our fate.
If fate does not split the love, people win their victory,
But nothing else besides—and nothing above, either.
These are the limits of man.

I sometimes wake at night—and at once my consciousness
is with you. I ask myself, If I could
take your freezing hands, warm them with my hands
—a unity will emerge, a vision of new existence,
which will embrace us both. Will it not die later, though?
I struggle so for hours, unable to sleep till morning,
tempted to escape somewhere—but I can't anymore.
We must go together from now on, Monica, we must go
      together,
even though I were to go away from you as early as my father
      left Mother.

All that we must leave behind and make our fate from
       scratch.
Love is a constant challenge, thrown to us by God,
thrown, I think, so that we should challenge fate.

MONICA

We must go together from now on. Christopher, we must go
       together,
even though I might become a stranger to you, like my mother
       to Father.
I was long afraid of love for this very reason. Today
I am still afraid of love, of that challenge to man.
You are taking a difficult girl, sensitive to a fault,
who easily withdraws into herself, and only with effort breaks
       the circle
constantly created by her "ego." You are taking a girl who
       absorbs
more than you can give, perhaps, and herself gives most
       sparingly.
Mother has more than once rebuked me for all this—and it is
       true.
I see it now more clearly and sharply even than she.

CHRISTOPHER

I cannot go beyond you. One does not love a person
for his "easy character." Why does one love at all?
What do I love you for, Monica? Don't ask me to answer.

I couldn't say. Love outdistances its object,
or approaches it so closely that it is almost lost from view.
Man must then think differently, must leave cold deliberations
—and in that "hot thinking" one question is important: Is it
    creative?
But even that he cannot tell, since he is so close to his object.
When the wave of emotion subsides, what remains will be
    important.

All this is true, Monica. And do you know what gives me
    most joy?
That there is so much truth in us that somehow we read
ordinary things more easily from the heart of these exultations.

3.

TERESA

That evening I could not help realizing, Andrew,
how heavily we all weigh upon their fate.
Take Monica's heritage: the rift of that love
is so deeply embedded in her that her own love
stems from a rift too. Christopher tries to heal it.
In him your love for me has endured, but also your absence
—the fear of love for someone absent. But this is no fault of
    ours.

We have become for them a threshold which they cannot
    cross without effort,

to reach their new homes—the homes of their own souls.
It is well, at least, if they do not stumble—
   We live in them for a very long time.
When they grow up under our eyes, they seem to become
      inaccessible,
like impermeable soil, but they have already absorbed us.
And though outwardly they shut themselves off,
inwardly we remain in them
and—a frightful thought—their lives somehow test
our own creation, our own suffering
(how else can one talk of love in the past tense?).

Here is the place where we once stood, just as they
are standing today. We looked into the window of that strange
      shop.
Certain truths do not pass, but continually return to people.
That truth, which years ago embodied itself in our life,
today embodies itself in them—

I must go up to them and say,
"Good evening, Monica; good evening, Christopher"
(I remember how once, Andrew, you stood here by me,
so discreetly: first I saw your face in the windowpane,
and only then felt your presence).
Andrew, nothing has passed—
I must go up to them and say this:
"My children, nothing has ceased to be, man must return
to the place from which his existence grows"—
and how strongly he desires it to grow through love.

                  .   .   .

And I know that the old jeweler, who tonight
is also older by these twenty-seven years,
gave you the same look, as if he were sounding your hearts
and defining through those rings a new level of existence . . .
Is the old jeweler's life changed into small pieces,
by being filled with the lives of people, the lives of so many,
        so many people.
Andrew took his ring and died with it,
I wear mine still—

CHRISTOPHER

When we took the rings I felt your hand trembling . . .
We forgot to pay attention to the face of that old man,
whom Mother told me about: his eyes are said to be very
        expressive.
It is not our fault that we read nothing
in his eyes; and he said little—things we knew anyway.
So do not be surprised, Mother, that his words left no trace
(things we knew anyway—we did not sense greatness),
and Monica's trembling hands told me much more.
I was engrossed in her being moved, and in my own
experience of her being moved, which I shared fully
—and I saw us two deep down in our experience:
I think I love her very much.

MONICA

We were taken up with each other—how could we tear
        ourselves away . . .

He did nothing to fascinate us . . .
he simply measured, first, the circumference of our fingers,
        then of the rings,
as an ordinary craftsman would. There was no artistry in it
        even.
He did not bring us closer to anything. All the beauty
        remained
in our own feeling. He did not widen or narrow anything
. . . I was absorbed by my love—and by nothing else, it seems.

TERESA

This frightened me, however . . . Does the old jeweler
not act anymore with the force of his eyes and his word?
Or is it that those two are unable to feel that force,
hidden in his look and his speech. Is it that they are different?

I said "Good evening" to them and shortly the conversation
        turned
to the wedding. Monica soon mentioned
her parents. They were absent in spirit.
Monica's love grew outside them, or even
in spite of them—that is what she thought. I, however,
knew that it grew out of that base which they
had left in her.
Monica was not ashamed of that rift, which of itself
was healing in their souls, and still had its echo in her.

What are you building, children? What cohesion
are these feelings of yours going to have beyond the old
        jeweler's message,

of which the vertical axis cuts across
every marriage in this world?

MONICA

I think about my parents, I think about my parents—
Since, of course, I try to imagine
our wedding day, Christopher, I often rehearse it.
It must be like rehearsals in a theater:
the theater of my imagination and the theater of my thought.
Father will play the part of father and the part of spouse,
and Mother will accept that part and adjust her own to it.
I shall be tired of their faces . . .
    Ah, when are we going to begin
to live our own lives at last! And when at last shall I believe
that you are not like Father! When will you be only
        Christopher
—free from those associations! I want so much to be yours,
and there is only one thing constantly in my way—that I am
        myself.

CHRISTOPHER

It was strange, dearest Mother, the story of my love
for Monica—whom I had to win over for herself,
and also for her parents (they do not really like me,
though things may be a bit better now . . .),
and yet I tried to imagine with her
their participation in our wedding:

after all, it is different from what you think, and will be
    different—
people have their depths, not only the masks on their faces.
Monica, what do you know about your mother's depths, and
    your father's—Stefan's?
When the day of our wedding comes,
you will emerge from between them—
once they both led a little girl by the hands,
and earlier still you were a baby
and your father came back from work
and asked your mother—Anna—
whether you had gained weight, Monica, and whether your
    appetite was good,
and was happy for every ounce of your little body,
was happy at your sleep, then at your chatter
—and in the process became a child himself.
All that cannot pass
without leaving a trace.

So when the day of our wedding comes,
I will come and take you away from them
a human being ripe for pain,
for the new pain of love,
for the pain of a new birth,
and we shall all be so intensely joyful
and we shall all stand on the border
of what in human language must be called "happiness."

Christopher, my son, is good to Monica,
as if he wanted to be to her the father he himself never knew
and the father she thought she had lost—
(a most strange process, Monica: when someone escapes from
      within us,
someone who exists, so he escapes only because we are not
      holding on to him—
an even stranger process: when by intuition
we create in ourselves a person who does not exist.
It is how Christopher created you, Andrew,
and still wants to create Stefan and Anna, Monica's parents,
      in her).

4.

When the day of their wedding came, both parents were there
and Monica stood between them in a white dress.
And Christopher walked next to me, Adam taking the place
      of his father.

Adam was the last person to see Andrew.
They had served in the same company. When Adam returned
      from the front,
he visited me at once and told me what Andrew had said.
Maybe Adam even took into his heart something of Andrew's
      great loves,

for Adam came to love Christopher dearly, and the boy had an
        affection for him.
I often found them at home deep in passionate conversation.
Adam did not grudge the time; he replaced the boy's father.

I was a bit uneasy, thinking that maybe he had me in mind
and would eventually ask for my hand. But one day he said,
"I am here, I suppose, to take up every man's future fate,
because his previous fate also had its roots in me."
I did not understand these words at all, but I know that since
        then
I have been totally at ease . . .

We were now very festive; Monica looked lovely,
and Christopher was somewhat pale. They were walking
        slowly toward each other.
Then Christopher took her by the arm and they walked ahead.
(The jeweler's shop was on their right as they half turned back
The young people exchanged rings—and left,
holding each other by the hand.
We stayed behind . . .)

I remember—the window of that shop once had become a
        strange mirror,
absorbing our future up to the point where
mystery began. Mystery, the unknown?
For us that was enough. Love was stronger than fear.
And today they went ahead. They did not even look at their
        reflection

in the mirror of that strange window, did not sound out the
      future.
Will the mystery, the unknown, begin at once for them?
As they were walking, Christopher clasped her arm. He
      wanted
to remold the memories of her parents.

5.

They have remained here, and I with Adam. Was I to
      examine
my Christopher's intuition?

ANNA

I never thought I would meet you here, Adam.
Perhaps even now this name sounds strange on my lips.
Do you remember? Once you unexpectedly started a
      conversation with me
right here—
You said to me, "The Bridegroom will pass down this
      street . . ."
I waited loitering for a while among the sleeping girls
while others carried lanterns and walked to meet him.
I went with them. When he came, I looked closely into his
      face.
It was Stefan's face. I wanted to run away at once.

. . .

Do you think I have reconciled myself to this even now?
A sense of disproportion did not vanish without trace.
I could not, cannot bring both these faces nearer,
I cannot identify them.

The old girlish love for that man dried up,
like water which cannot a second time spring from the earth.
I tried, though, to believe in him, and in an order,
in an order governing everything, including my own life.
Besides—I ceased to despise him, ceased to bear a grudge,
that terrible grudge at my life which he had wasted.
I began to look for guilt in myself as well. It was there.
I did not now cut conversations short. Did not keep silent to
        crush him.
Did he change? I do not know. But he became less
        burdensome.
He too must have found it easier to bear my presence.
We may have stopped moving away from each other at such
        a pace
as before. Now things seem to stand still.
Do we live through each other? I suppose not. We live more
        through our children.
Monica is the most difficult; it is in her that we destroyed most.
Now she is leaving us. To my mind, too early
—and she is taking with her a certainty of her parents' guilt
(in this, I suppose, she does us wrong).

That the Bridegroom had to have Stefan's face—this I now
        understand.

But I became one of the foolish virgins, one who has no more
    oil
and whose lamp burns badly, using up in the process nearly
    every
fiber of my soul.

ADAM

    That evening I saw Anna again. The memory of her en-
counter with the Bridegroom was still vivid to her. Anna had
entered the road of complementary love. She had to comple-
ment, giving and taking in different proportions than before.
The turning point occurred that night many years ago. At that
time everything threatened destruction. A new love could begin
only through a meeting with the Bridegroom. What Anna
felt of it at first was only the suffering. In the course of time a
gradual calm came. And something new that was growing, was
still intangible, and, above all, did not "taste" of love. One
day they may learn to relish the taste of that something new
. . . At any rate, Anna is closer to it than Stefan.
    The cause lies in the past. The error resides simply there.
The thing is that love carries people away like an *absolute*,
although it lacks absolute dimensions. But acting under an
illusion, they do not try to connect that love with the Love that
has such a dimension. They do not even feel the need, blinded
as they are not so much by the force of their emotion as by
lack of humility. They lack humility toward what love must
be in its true essence. The more aware they are of it, the
smaller the danger. Otherwise the danger is great: love will
not stand the pressure of reality.

Ah, how sorry I was for Anna that night many years ago, how sorry I was for Stefan. They already had three children, who were beginning to grow up (Monica felt everything most strongly). I was terribly sorry for them—much more even than for Andrew, when he was taking leave of me on the way to his outpost; he said then, "I shan't come back." It remained for me to take that news to the widow and orphan. I tried to take the place of father for Christopher, since I had not been able to take Andrew's place in dying.

Sometimes human existence seems too short for love. At other times it is, however, the other way around: human love seems too short in relation to existence—or rather, too trivial. At any rate, every person has at his disposal an existence and a Love. The problem is: How to build a sensible structure from it?

But this structure must never be inward-looking. It must be open in such a way that on the one hand it embraces other people, while on the other, it always reflects the absolute Existence and Love; it must always, *in some way*, reflect them.

That, too, is the ultimate sense of your lives:

Teresa!
Andrew!
Anna!
Stefan!

and yours:

Monica!
Christopher!

Adam mentioned us one by one. Left his own name out.
He was, as it were, a common denominator of us all,
at the same time a spokesman and a judge.
Somehow we quietly entrusted ourselves to his thoughts, his
analysis
and heart.
All this—all this was, and moved, or was moving slowly
into another structure.
It was hard to tear thought and heart away from the young
ones:
Monica and Christopher again reflect *in some way*
the absolute Existence and Love.
How? This is the question one cannot ask
to its conclusion.
(The mirror where I had seen the immediate future with
Andrew wasn't even there.)
Ah, the jeweler has locked up his shop. And the two young
people have both gone away.
Do they know at least what they reflect? Should one not
follow them?
But, after all, they have their own thoughts . . .
They will come back here, they will certainly come back.
They have simple gone to ponder for a while:
to create something, to reflect the absolute Existence and Love,
must be the most wonderful of all!

But one lives in ignorance of it.

I, too, did not seem to know what Adam, and then Teresa, Christopher's mother, were talking about. Earlier, Anna had seemed to make a confession to Adam about many of the later years of her life. When she had finished talking about the Bridegroom, who "must have had" my face, she immediately referred to Monica. That was the one thing I understood best: Monica wants to leave us at any price—why, why?

I do not understand what it means "to reflect the absolute Existence and Love"—but if Monica wants so much to go away from us, then I know for certain that it is because of that: we both of us, Anna and I, reflect them very badly. This I have understood clearly, and it somehow hurts me too.

Also at this moment—for the first time in many years—I felt the need to say something that would open up my soul, to say it to Anna (this was an attempt at self-accusation, or rather, an attempt to divide the guilt between us two).

At any rate, I have come up to her and put my hand on her shoulder (something I have not done for a long, long time). I have also said these words:

"What a pity that for so many years we have not felt ourselves to be a couple of children.

"Anna, Anna, how much we have lost because of that!"

About the Author

KAROL WOJTYLA—Pope John Paul II—has long been involved with the theater. As a student of literature, then priest, bishop and archbishop, he acted, directed, wrote dramatic criticism, made a Polish translation of Sophocles' *Oedipus*, helped found the Rhapsodic Theater—an underground group that staged inspirational poems and plays during the years of Nazi occupation—and himself authored six plays. *The Jeweler's Shop*— written when he was Bishop of Krakow—first appeared in 1960 in a Polish Catholic monthly under Wojtyla's literary pseudonym, Andrzej Jawien.

About the Translator

BOLESLAW TABORSKI was born and raised in Poland, where, as a student in wartime Krakow, he was closely involved with the underground theater. Since the end of the war he has lived in Great Britain, going in 1947 to Bristol University to study English philology and drama. A poet, critic and translator, he has been widely published in England, the United States and Poland. He was chosen as translator of *The Jeweler's Shop* by a special Papal Commission.